Chinese Designs

Dianne Gaspas

DOVER PUBLICATIONS, INC.
Mineola, NewYork

PUBLISHER'S NOTE

The images presented by Dianne Gaspas in *Chinese Designs* derive from the vast vocabulary of traditional Chinese design motifs. For the most part these are characteristic motifs that have been used in textile embroidery, painting, ceramics, bronze, lacquer, and other crafts.

Many motifs have some symbolic significance: mandarin ducks signify marital bliss; cranes, longevity; the lotus, purity; the peony, wealth and honor; plum blossoms, spring; bats happiness or good fortune; lions, strength. The dragon is the symbol of China itself, and of imperial power; the phoenix represents peace, good fortune and feminine beauty. It is considered the female counterpart of the dragon.

Copyright

Copyright © 2002 by Dover Publications, Inc.
All rights reserved under Pan American and International Copyright Conventions.

Bibliographical Note

Chinese Designs is a new work, first published by Dover Publications, Inc., in 2002.

DOVER *Pictorial Archive* SERIES

This book belongs to the Dover Pictorial Archive Series. You may use the designs and illustrations for graphics and crafts applications, free and without special permission, provided that you include no more than four in the same publication or project. (For permission for additional use, please write to Permissions Department, Dover Publications, Inc., 31 East 2nd Street, Mineola, N.Y. 11501.)

However, republication or reproduction of any illustration by any other graphic service, whether it be in a book or in any other design resource, is strictly prohibited.

International Standard Book Number: 0-486-42083-3

Manufactured in the United States of America
Dover Publications, Inc., 31 East 2nd Street, Mineola, N.Y. 11501

1. **Dragon**. Embroidery design for the front of a dragon robe. From an opera costume.

2. **Dragon.** Embroidery design for a court robe.

3. **Dragon.** A traditional motif for an embroidered badge.

4. **Cranes.** Design for a porcelain vase or plate.

5. **Lions.** Design for porcelain.

6. **Lion.** Design for a plate or medallion.

7. **Crane.** Embroidery design for the front, back, and sleeves of a woman's informal robe. From an opera costume.

8. **Crane.** Embroidery design for the front, back, and sleeves of an official's crane robe. From an opera costume.

9. **Crane.** Embroidery design for the front, back, and sleeves of an informal robe. From an opera costume.

10. **Partridge.** Design for a porcelain vase or plate.

11. **Mandarin ducks.** Design for a porcelain vase or plate.

12. **Mandarin ducks and lotus.** Embroidery design for the front, back, and sleeves of a woman's informal robe. From an opera costume.

13. **Mandarin ducks and lotus.** Embroidery design for the front, back, and sleeves of a woman's informal robe. From an opera costume.

14. **Cherries.** Design for a medallion in lacquer.

15. **Lilies.** Design for a medallion in lacquer.

16. **Peony**. Embroidery design for the front, back, and sleeves of an informal robe. From an opera costume.

17. **Peony and plum blossoms** with bird. Embroidery design for the front, back, and sleeves of a woman's informal robe. From an opera costume.

18. **Landscape.** A river- or lakeside scene.

19. **Grasshoppers.** Design for porcelain vase or plate.

20. **Fish.** Embroidery design for the hanging border of a warrior's tunic. From an opera costume.

21. **Bats among clouds**, representing blessings from heaven. Embroidery design for the front and back of a traveling garment. From an opera costume.

22. **Butterflies.** Design for a porcelain vase or plate.

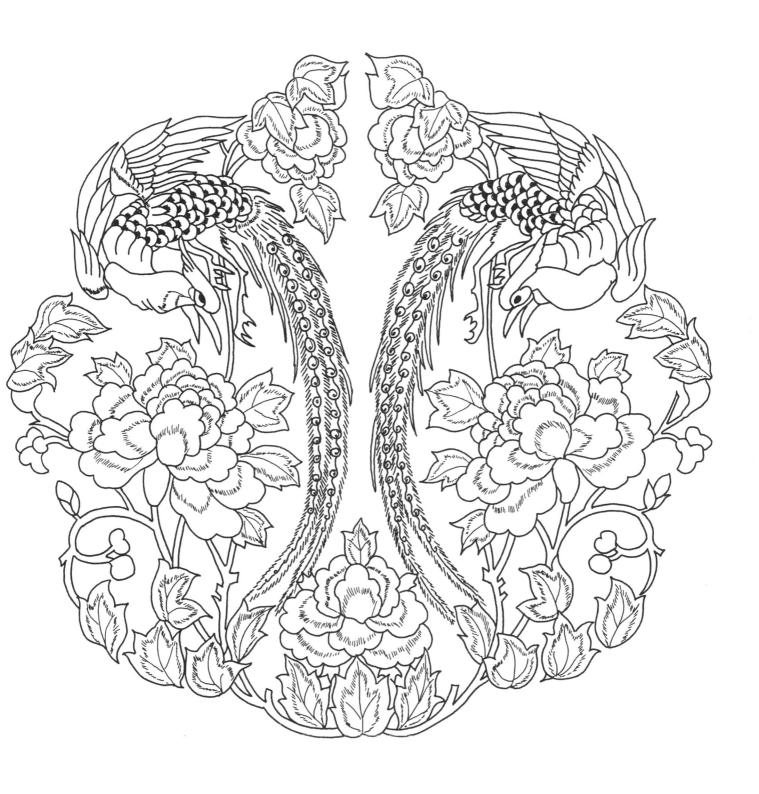

23. **Phoenixes and peonies**. Embroidery design for the front, back, and sleeves of a woman's informal robe. From an opera costume.

24. **Phoenix and flowers.** Embroidery design for the front and back, of a woman's informal robe. From an opera costume.

25. **Phoenixes.** Design for porcelain vase or plate.

26. **Phoenix.** Embroidery design for the front, back and sleeves of a woman's informal robe. From an opera costume.

27. **Phoenix.** Embroidery design for the front and back of a woman's ordinary robe. From an opera costume.

28. **Phoenix.** Embroidery design for the front and back of a woman's
informal robe. From an opera costume.

29. **Phoenix.** Embroidery design for the front, back, and sleeves of a woman's informal robe. From an opera costume.

30. **Phoenix.** Embroidery design for the front, back, and sleeves of a woman's informal robe. From an opera costume.